MY BODY

Angela
Royston

Sally
Hewitt

QEB Publishing

Copyright © QEB Publishing, Inc. 2010
3 Wrigley, Suite A
Irvine, CA 92618

First published in the United States by
QEB Publishing, Inc.
3 Wrigley, Suite A
Irvine, CA 92618

www.qed-publishing.co.uk

A catalogue record for this book is available
from the Library of Congress.

ISBN 978 1 59566 869 1 (paperback)

Printed in China

Consultant Terry Jennings
Project Editor Judith Millidge
Designer Kim Hall
Picture Researcher Claudia Tate
Illustrator Chris Davidson

Words in **bold** are explained in the Glossary on page 44.

Contents

What is your heart?

Your heart is a strong **muscle** about the size of your fist. It has two pumps that push your **blood** around your body. Your heart sits just to the left of the middle of your chest.

Heart shapes are everywhere, on balloons, cards, and cuddly toys. But your real heart looks quite different.

Your heart never stops working. It **pumps** your blood all day and all night to every part of your body. Your **brain**, lungs, skin, and muscles need blood to work properly.

A doctor uses a stethoscope to listen to your heart.

Your heart doesn't work as hard when you are asleep. When you wake up and start moving it beats faster.

Veins and arteries

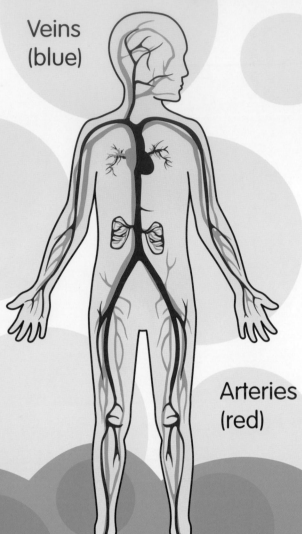

Veins
(blue)

Arteries
(red)

Your heart pumps your blood into tubes called **blood vessels**. Blood vessels called arteries carry blood away from your heart to every other part of your body. Blood vessels called veins bring blood back to your heart.

When you exercise, your body warms up and sometimes your skin turns red. This is because blood rushes to the blood vessels in your skin to keep you cool.

6

Around and around

Your blood is always moving around your body and through your heart. This movement is called circulation. It takes less than a minute for your heart to pump blood to every part of your body!

Activity

You can *see* blood flowing through your hand. Hold your right hand in the air for a few moments. Hang your left hand down by your side.

Now look at the color of each hand. It is harder for your heart to pump blood upward, so your right hand looks pale because there is less blood in it.

Blood

Your blood is like a delivery truck. It carries **oxygen** from your lungs and goodness from your food to every part of your body.

Your blood is full of tiny cells, which carry the oxygen. These cells give your blood its red color.

If you fall and cut yourself, your blood dries into a hard scab and your skin heals underneath the scab.

Feel the beat

When you are working hard, if you are running for example, your body needs more oxygen from your blood, so your heart beats faster.

You can feel your heart beat in the blood vessels on your wrists. This is called your pulse.

Activity

Feel your pulse. Now run on the spot for a few moments. Feel your pulse again.

Your heart usually beats about 90 times a minute.

Your pulse gets faster when you work hard.

9

Lungs

Your lungs are the part of your body you **breathe** with. They are like two big sacks in your chest. Your left lung is a bit smaller than your right lung to make room for your heart.

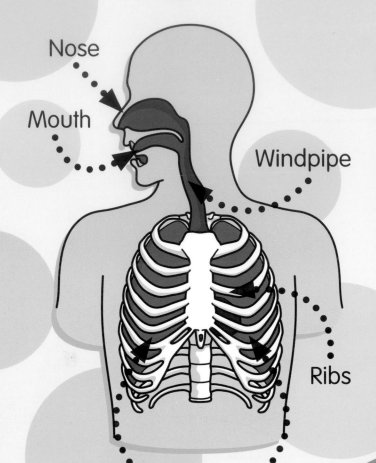

Nose

Mouth

Windpipe

Ribs

Lungs

The insides of your lungs are like sponges. They soak up air instead of water.

Ribs

Lung muscle that squeezes air in and out.

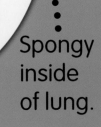

Spongy inside of lung.

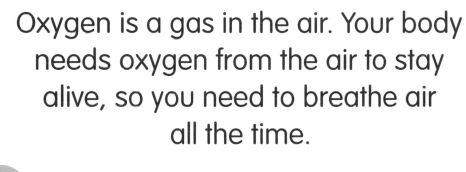

Oxygen is a gas in the air. Your body needs oxygen from the air to stay alive, so you need to breathe air all the time.

Humans can't breathe under water, unless they use a tube called a snorkel while swimming.

Healthy heart and lungs

Look after your heart and lungs. Keeping active makes your heart and lungs work harder. Hard work makes them strong and healthy so they can help to keep your whole body healthy.

Healthy eating

You can help protect your heart, blood vessels, and lungs by eating fresh food, lots of fruit and vegetables, and not too much fat, salt, or sugar.

Healthy food is good for you and delicious, too!

Fresh air

Fresh air is good for your lungs. Sometimes the air in big cities is polluted by fumes from cars. Polluted air is bad for you because it contains tiny bits of smoke and dust that make you cough.

Take a trip to the countryside or to the shore where the air is fresh and clean.

Sleep

When you are asleep your brain makes sure you keep breathing in and out during the night.

When you wake up after a good night's sleep, you are rested and ready for a busy day.

13

What is your skeleton?

Your skeleton is like a strong frame. It gives your body its **shape**, holds you upright, and lets you move. It **protects** soft parts of your body, such as your heart and lungs.

Your skeleton is made up of bones of different shapes and sizes. Each bone has a job to do.

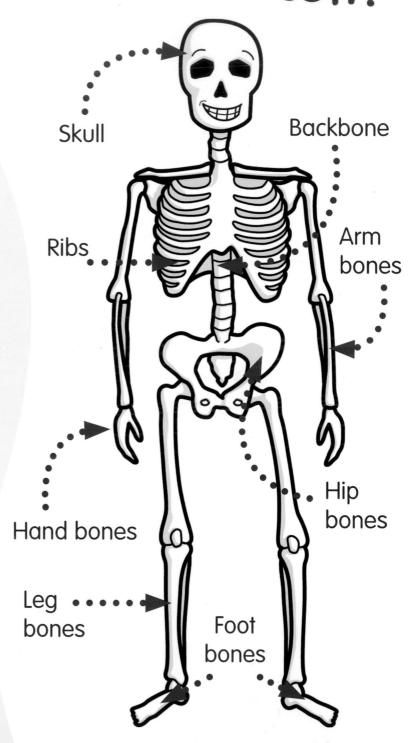

Skull

Backbone

Ribs

Arm bones

Hip bones

Hand bones

Leg bones

Foot bones

Your body is **alive** and growing, and so are your bones. As you grow older, your bones become harder and stronger. By the time you are fully grown, you will have 206 bones.

A baby has tiny hands and feet and soft, bendy bones.

Activity

Which of your bones can you feel through your skin?

Can you feel the top of the bone in your upper arm? Your ribs?

15

Your bones

Your bones need to be strong and light. Bones are light enough to let you jump, and strong enough not to break when you land.

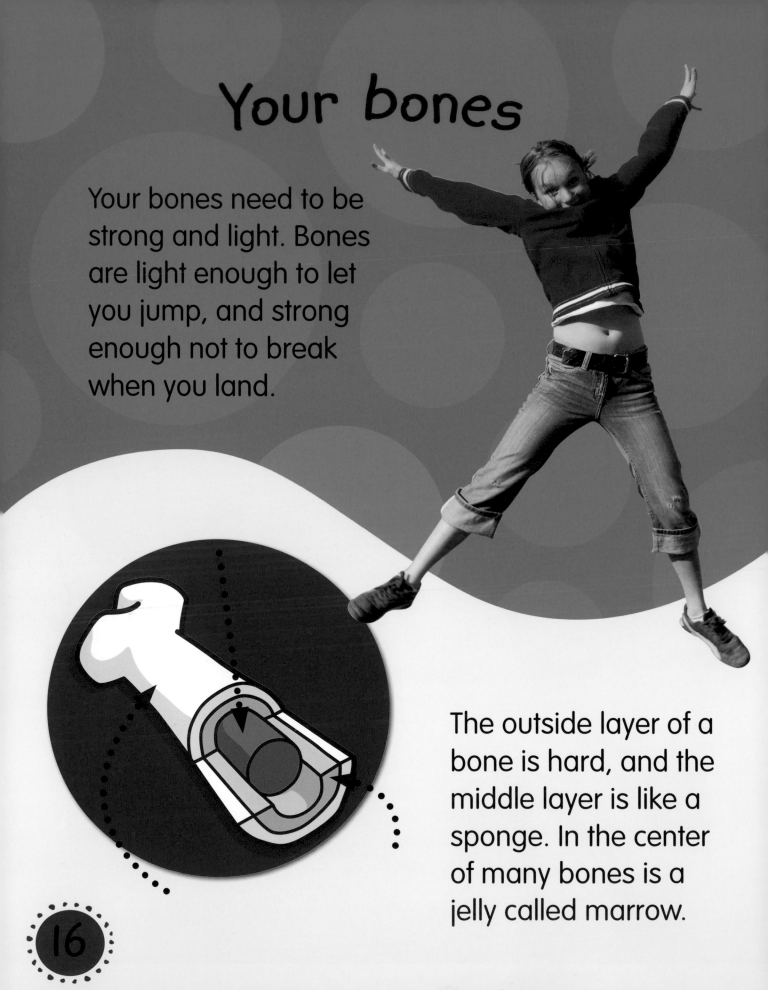

The outside layer of a bone is hard, and the middle layer is like a sponge. In the center of many bones is a jelly called marrow.

16

Even though bones are very strong, they sometimes break. Bones are amazing! They can fix themselves and become just as strong again.

It usually takes about six weeks for a broken bone to mend.

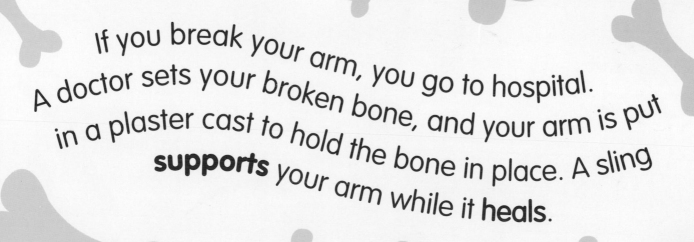

If you break your arm, you go to hospital. A doctor sets your broken bone, and your arm is put in a plaster cast to hold the bone in place. A sling **supports** your arm while it **heals**.

Healthy bones

Just like the rest of your body, your bones need plenty of good food and **exercise**, as well as rest and sleep.

Milk, eggs, cheese, and yoghurt, tinned salmon, and sardines, as well as leafy, green vegetables all help keep your bones strong and healthy.

Whatever exercise you enjoy, such as running, dancing, or ball games, will keep you active and help your bones to grow strong.

Do something active every day.

Wear a helmet when you ride a bicycle to protect your skull. Wear pads to protect your knees and elbows when you skate.

You can have fun and look after your bones!

19

Your skull

Your **skull** is made up of several bones. It is very strong. Its most important job is to protect your brain. Feel the shape of your skull. It has two holes for your eyes. Your jaw opens and closes when you talk and also when you eat.

The top of your skull is exactly the right shape and size to cover and protect your brain.

The bones in your skull give your face its shape. We all have a forehead, eyes, nose, a mouth, and a chin. Everyone looks just a bit different so we can recognize each other easily.

It would be very confusing if we all looked exactly the same.

Activity

Look in the mirror and draw a picture of your face. Then, draw your friend's face. Which parts of the drawings look the same and which look different?

Your backbone

Spine

Your backbone, or "spine," runs right down the middle of your back. It is made up of 26 small bones. If it were made of just one long bone, you would not be able to bend or twist.

Activity

Bend your knees, curl your back, and touch your toes, then stand up again. Feel your backbone bend and straighten up again.

Your backbone holds you upright. If you stand, walk, and sit with a straight back, your spine supports your whole body.

Gymnasts hold their backs straight to help them balance.

23

What is your digestive system?

When you eat, your food goes on a journey through your **digestive system**.

On the way, your body takes nutrients (the bits that are good for you) from the food. Then, your body gets rid of the bits it can't use.

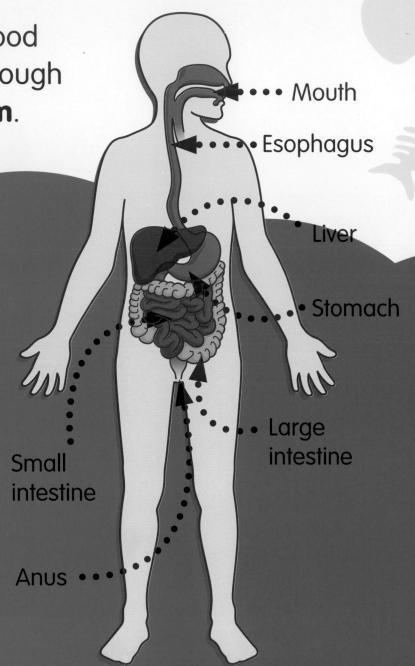

Mouth

Esophagus

Liver

Stomach

Small intestine

Large intestine

Anus

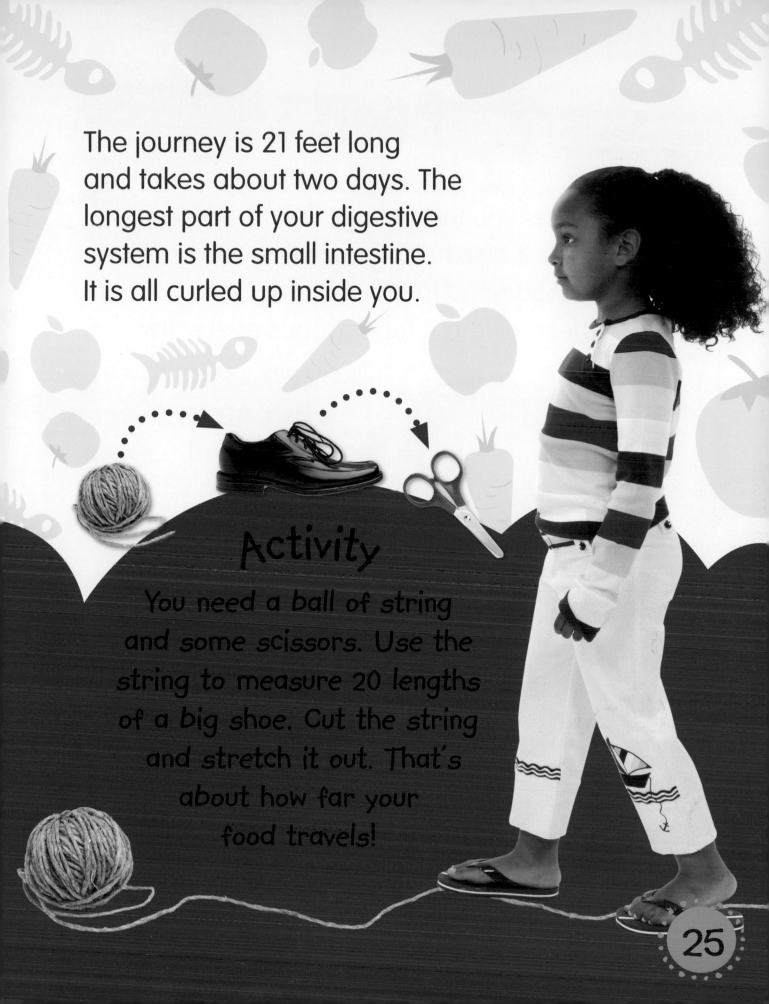

The journey is 21 feet long and takes about two days. The longest part of your digestive system is the small intestine. It is all curled up inside you.

Activity

You need a ball of string and some scissors. Use the string to measure 20 lengths of a big shoe. Cut the string and stretch it out. That's about how far your food travels!

Food

Food gives you the **energy** you need to work and grow. It also helps you to keep warm and healthy. You need to eat something from each of these different food groups every day.

Fish, meat, eggs, and nuts help your body to grow and heal.

Bread, cereal, and pasta give you the energy you need to keep you going all day.

Milk, cheese, butter, and cream help to build strong bones and give you energy.

Fruit and vegetables are full of **vitamins** and **minerals** that help to keep you healthy. They are full of fiber, the rough part of food that helps your body to get rid of waste.

You only need a little sugar and salt in your food, but it is important to drink plenty of water.

27

Stomach

Your esophagus pushes food into your stomach. Your stomach is a muscle. It is like a stretchy bag. It stretches when it is full of food.

Food stays in your stomach for about three hours while it is digested. "Digested" means that it is mixed and mashed up.

After a big meal, you feel full.

When your food has turned soft and runny like soup, it leaves your stomach. You start to feel **hungry** again when your stomach is empty.

Activity

Make a timetable of your meals. Notice the time when you feel hungry. Is it about three hours after your last meal? A healthy snack can stop you feeling hungry between meals.

Breakfast	8 o'clock
Lunch	1 o'clock
Dinner	6 o'clock

Small intestine

Your food takes about four hours to ooze along your small intestine where it becomes even more runny and watery. Bubbles of gas in your intestines make a rumbling sound while your food is being digested.

Activity

Listen to tummy rumbles. When a friend's or one of your family's tummy rumbles loudly, ask if you can put your ear on their stomach and listen to their food being digested!

Food is full of "nutrients," or goodness, that your body needs to grow, stay healthy, and to give you energy. While your food is in your small intestine, nutrients from your food go into your blood.

It's important to eat food full of the nutrients your body needs.

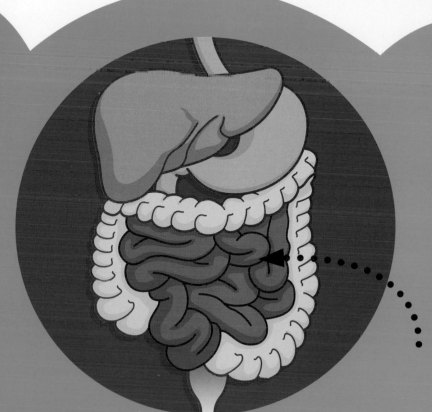

Your small intestine is longer than your large intestine. It is called small because it is narrow.

Small intestine

Large intestine

Your food finally travels from your small intestine into your large intestine. There, water goes into your blood. Everything else passes out of your body.

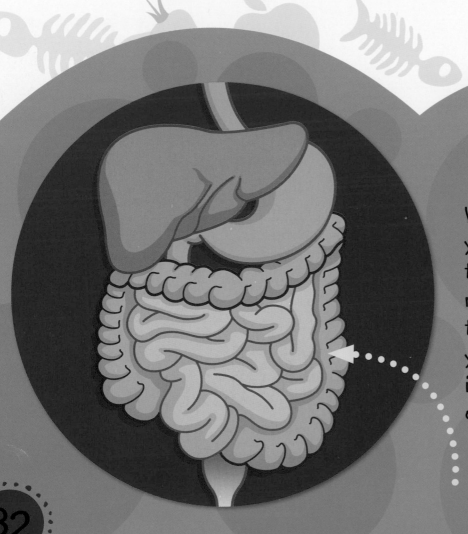

While your food is in your large intestine, the last little bit of nutrients and most of the water goes into your body. Your food is nearly at the end of its journey.

Large intestine

When your food reaches the large intestine, it is mostly waste. Waste is the part of your food that your body doesn't need. It goes into the large intestine and stays there for about two days.

Your body gets rid of your waste when you go to the bathroom. Always remember to wash your hands afterward!

33

Your brain

Your brain is kept safe inside a strong bone in your head called your skull. Your brain needs to be protected because it is soft.

Your skull is just the right size and shape for your brain to sit inside. Your skull is made up of two sets of bones. The bones of your face are in one set and the other set protects your brain.

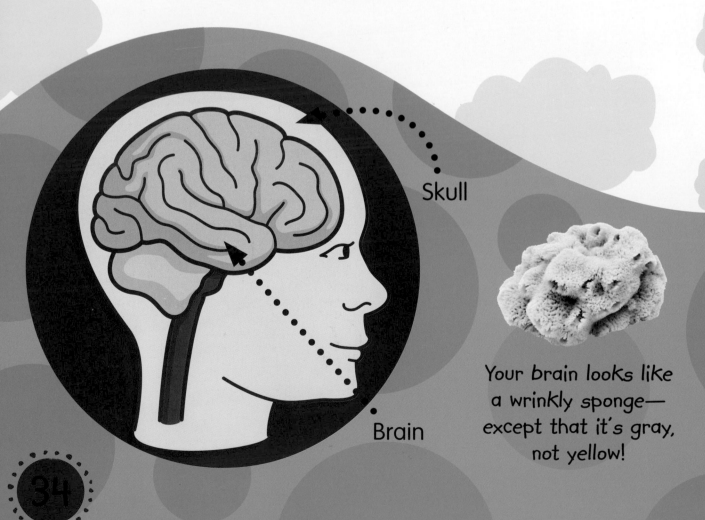

Skull

Brain

Your brain looks like a wrinkly sponge—except that it's gray, not yellow!

Every part of your brain has a job to do.

You think with the biggest part of your brain.

The brain stem controls **digestion** and makes sure your heart and breathing never stop, even when you are asleep.

The back of your brain controls how you move.

Nerves

Nerves carry **messages** from your brain to every part of your body and back again. Your nerves are like pathways.

Your spinal cord is a long tube of nerves down the middle of your back. The nerves in your spinal cord link your brain to every part of your body.

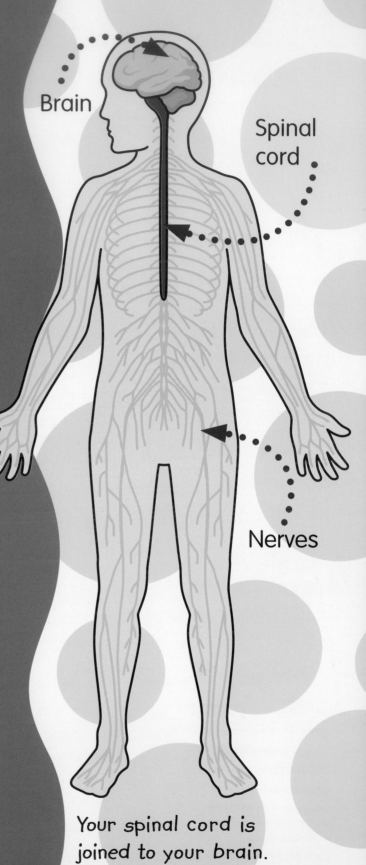

Brain

Spinal cord

Nerves

Your spinal cord is joined to your brain.

Two kinds of messages are sent along your nerves. One goes to your brain to tell it what is happening. The brain sends a reply to tell your body how to react.

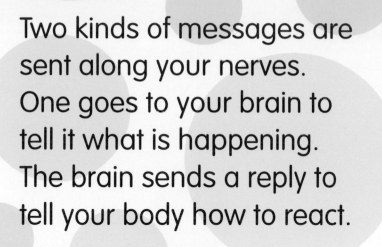

This feels wet...

Pull hand out of water to get dry.

Feel something soft, such as the fur of a cat. One message tells your brain, "This feels soft!" The message that comes back tells your arm to move and your hand to stroke the cat gently.

37

Senses

Your **senses** tell you what is going on around you. You have five senses.

You *see* with your eyes.
You *hear* with your ears.
You *smell* with your nose.
You *taste* with your tongue.
You *feel* with your skin.

apple!

When you see something, a message is sent along your nerves from your eyes to your brain.

Your brain tells you what you are seeing.

Your senses work together to tell you things.

Your eyes see flames, your nose smells smoke, your ears hear crackling, and your brain tells you "Fire!"

Your skin feels hot and warns you, "Don't touch!"

Activity

Can you tell what something is by only using one sense?

Smell an orange, soap, chocolate, and a flower. Now feel them as well.

Does that help?

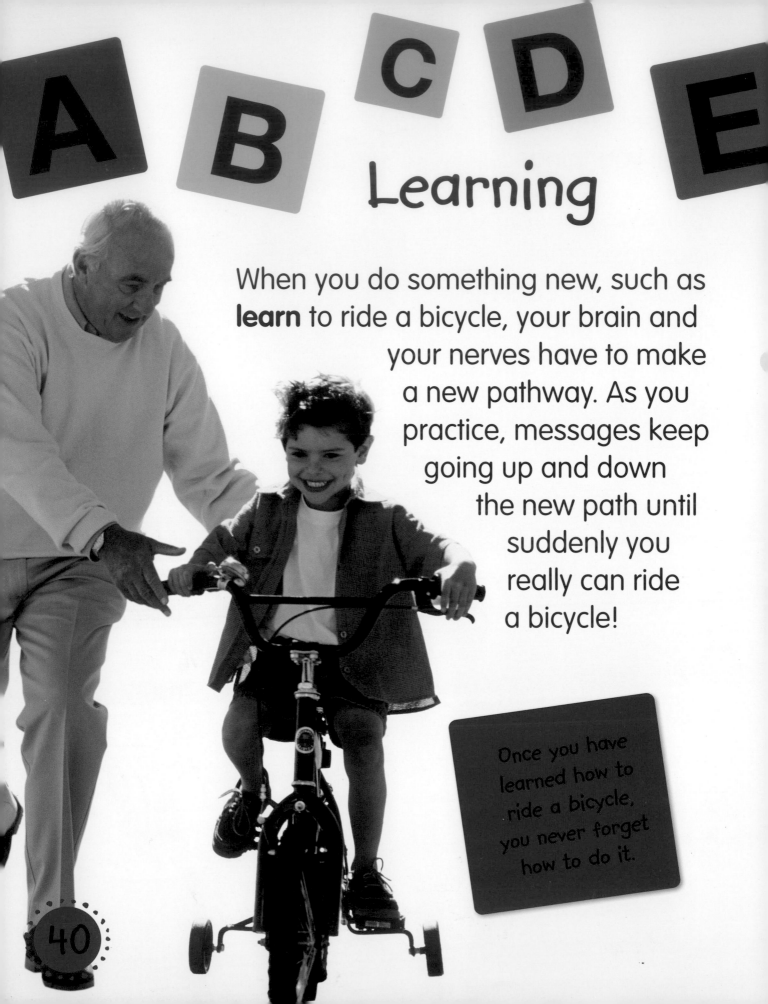

Learning

When you do something new, such as **learn** to ride a bicycle, your brain and your nerves have to make a new pathway. As you practice, messages keep going up and down the new path until suddenly you really can ride a bicycle!

Once you have learned how to ride a bicycle, you never forget how to do it.

Hard work and practice help you to learn new things, **remember** how to do them, and get better at doing them.

Write your name with the hand you don't usually use. Practice over and over. Do you get better at writing with the "wrong" hand?

Feelings

How do you feel when you have been invited to a sleepover with your friends? How do you feel if someone borrows your favorite pen—then loses it? Do you feel excited, angry, sad, happy?

You can usually tell how someone is feeling by the look on their face.

Your feelings come from your brain.

Activity

With your friend, think of a feeling, then pull a face and make your body show that feeling. Can your friend guess what the feeling is just by looking at you?

Feelings can help you to do the right thing at the right time.

If you feel afraid of a scary animal, you keep away from it.

BEWARE OF THE DOG

If you feel happy to see your friend, you smile and your friend smiles back. You both feel happy and have a good time.

Glossary

Alive
You are alive, and so are plants and animals. Things that are alive grow, move, eat, and can sense what is going on around them.

Blood
Blood is the red liquid that runs through your blood vessels to every part of your body. It carries goodness from your food and oxygen from your lungs.

Blood vessels
Blood vessels are tubes that carry your blood. Arteries are blood vessels that carry blood away from your heart. Veins are blood vessels that carry blood back to your heart.

Bone
Bones are strong and light. The 206 bones in your body are joined together to make up your skeleton.

Brain
Your brain is inside your head. It is soft, gray, and wrinkly, and it is the part of your body that controls everything you do.

Breathe
You breathe air in and out of your lungs all the time. You breathe through your nose and mouth.

Digestion
When your body digests food, it mashes it up, uses the goodness, and gets rid of the waste.

Digestive system
Your digestive system is all the parts of your body that work together to digest your food.

Energy
Energy is what you need to give you the power to work. Food gives you energy.

Glossary

Exercise
Exercise is moving about, for example running, swimming, jumping, stretching, and skipping. Exercise helps to keep your body strong and healthy.

Heal
Your body heals or gets better when you cut yourself or when you are sick.

Hungry
You feel hungry when your stomach is empty. Feeling hungry makes you want to eat.

Learn
You learn when you discover something new and remember it. For example, you learn to read, or to ride a bike. And you learn new facts every day.

Messages
Messages are facts and information sent from one place to another. Messages are sent along your nerves to your brain. If you see a bird, a message goes from your eyes to your brain. Your brain tells you "bird!"

Minerals
Minerals are tiny parts of goodness in food. Minerals in milk help you build strong teeth and bones.

Muscles
Your muscles pull your bones so you can move. Muscles keep your heart beating and your lungs breathing.

Nerves
Your nerves are like pathways running from your brain to every part of your body. Messages are sent to and fro along your nerves.

Glossary

Oxygen
Oxygen is a gas in the air. Your lungs take oxygen from the air when you breathe in. Your blood carries oxygen from your lungs around your body.

Protect
"Protect" means to keep something safe from being hurt. Your skull protects your brain.

Pump
A pump pushes liquid along. Your heart is a pump that pushes blood through your blood vessels.

Remember
When you learn a new skill, you remember it. You don't forget it and you don't have to learn it again.

Senses
You have five senses—sight, touch, taste, smell, and hearing. They give you information about what is going on around you.

Skull
Your skull is the framework of bones in your head that protects your brain. It is sometimes called your brain box.

Shape
Everything has a shape. For example, a ball is a round shape. Your skeleton gives your body its shape.

Support
"Support" means to hold something upright or stop it from falling.

Vitamins
Vitamins are tiny parts of goodness in food. Vitamins in fruit help to keep your skin healthy.

Windpipe
Your windpipe is the tube that carries air into your lungs when you breathe in, and carries it out again when you breathe out.

Index

Notes for parents and teachers

1. Feel your ribs and breastbone. Discuss how your ribs protect your heart. Explain that your heart needs to be protected because it is soft. Use the word "muscle" and feel other muscles that let you move. Use the word "pump" and talk about how a pump pushes liquid.

2. Find the blood vessels in your wrist. Feel each other's pulse and explain that each beat is your heart pumping blood all around your body.

3. Run together on the spot and feel how your heart beats faster and you breather more quickly after exercise. Explain that this is because your body needs more oxygen when you work hard. Feel your heart beat and notice that your breathing slows down when you rest.

4. Talk about how we all need energy to give us the power to work and play, and that food gives us energy. Discuss other kinds of energy, such as petrol for cars, and electricity for light. What happens to us without food, to a card without petrol and to a light without electricity?

5. Talk about how the brain lets us sense the world around us. You can point to the parts of the body you use to see, hear, taste, smell, and touch. Think of one thing you learn to do using each of your senses.

6. Learn something new together, maybe a poem or a new activity, such as juggling or a tune on the recorder. Talk about what you find hard and what you find easy when learning something new.